LEAD *to* Follow

MARY GRIFFIN

Special thanks to Mrs. Katrina Black for
being the final editor of this book.

CONTENTS

PREFACE

When God instructed me to write this book, I was ecstatic. As I began to type what he was feeding me, I became lost and confused. The words and sentences did not fit the meaning of what I thought I was supposed to be writing. But that's what happens when you follow the leading of his will—because the Scripture says,

> But God hath chosen the foolish things of the world to confound the wise; and God hath chosen the weak things of the world to confound the things which are mighty. (1 Corinthians 1:27)

It's not our thoughts or our ways that is on display but his.

It is God's plan that all leaders remain humble. This was the bottom line to the whole shebang. So often leaders get lifted up in pride and fall from the assignment plan that God had intended for them to follow. The scripture says,

> Pride goeth before destruction, and a haughty spirit before a fall. (Proverbs 16:18)

Haven't you seen lots of negative news articles about leadership such as the following:

- Pastor allegedly stole $450k from federal summer food program
- Pastors charged with sex crimes
- Youth pastor removed and charged with peddling drugs in church youth camp

Not surprised? Of course, not, because more and more of these articles are popping up all over. What went wrong? What happened? What is leadership exemplifying? We are the light of the world, the salt of the earth. Well, what is the world going to do when we the church allow our light to go out and our salt to lose its savor?

The anointing and the appointment rest on obedience to God. It is mandatory to put your agenda aside and follow God's leading whether that leading is him talking directly to you or using someone else to be his mouthpiece to instruct you of his will. If you can't follow the instructions, you can't follow the fruit of the anointing and appointing. There is a process on this journey, and it all starts with following. If you decide to take a trip, you must start to travel on a road. That road you are traveling is filled with all kinds of signs that give you instructions to follow. Some of the instructions may be to

slow down,

be careful because of sharp turn

or of wild animals crossing,

come to a stop soon, or

inform of a bumpy road ahead.

If you don't heed the warning on the road signs, this is the sign that shows what position you will end up:

The bible says,

> He, that being often reproved hardeneth his
> neck, shall suddenly be destroyed, and that with-
> out remedy. (Proverbs 29:1)

When you follow God's leadership, always have in mind *Jeremiah 29:11*:

> For I know the thoughts that I think toward you,
> saith the LORD, thoughts of peace, and not of
> evil, to give you an expected end.

Trust God's leadership and follow.

INTRODUCTION

The title threw you for a loop! It seems to be turned around, but that's how God revealed it.

> But God hath chosen the foolish things of the
> world to confound the wise. (1 Corinthians 1:27)

Normally, the statement "Follow the leader" is quoted. That puts the leader in the driver's seat, and everyone else is a passenger. But in this book, God is placing the leader in the passenger's seat. Well, who is doing the driving? Well, of course, God. Since God has the license for everyone's lives, he has the ability to shift things around. In this instance, the leader is being taught to be a follower not just to get a leadership role, to continue to follow Him after the leadership role has been obtained. God can use the leader better that way. Why? If a leader puts his agenda last, then that opens the opportunity for God's agenda to be doing the leading. And we all know what happens when God's agenda is first.

> And we know that all things work together for
> good to them that love God, to them who are the
> called according to his purpose. (Romans 8:28)

So no, you are not confused as to what God is saying in this book. Your role as a leader is *following*.

What is leadership? *Merriam-Webster* defines it as "the office of a leader; the capacity to lead; the act or the instance of leading." Wikipedia defines leadership as "a process of social influence in which a person can enlist the aid and support of others in the accomplishment of a common task; some understand a leader simply as somebody people follow, or as somebody who guides or directs others; organizing a group of people to achieve a common goal." In this book, God defines leadership as the act and ability to follow. One must simply know how to follow to be a good leader. Having the ability and humble spirit to follow is not just the prerequisite of being a good leader, but it is the quality and characteristic of a leader that holds the leadership position. Strange, huh! You will see how the role of a leader is all about following. The aspect of good leadership means following in *spiritual things*; *dealing with people*; *making everyday decisions* that may affect the *church*, your *home*; and following in your own *personal life*. In leadership, *servitude* climbs to a higher level.

CHAPTER 1

Spiritual Things

How many times have you sat and meditated spiritually, and in that meditation, God gave you direction? That's why I am sitting at the computer right now, typing this book—because of God's direction. When you receive spiritual directions from God, your next step is to not lead but follow. Obeying God is an act of servitude. When Paul wrote his letters to the church, most of them began with him addressing himself as a servant—for example, *Romans 1:1*:

> Paul, a servant of Jesus Christ, called to be an apostle, separated unto the gospel of God.

Paul's use of the word *servant* is translated in the Strong's Greek Lexicon as "slave." Paul did not view slavery as a harsh dominant life, but he welcomed his commitment to the gospel. He followed God's direction on his journey. Yes, he preached the gospel in many countries and was the leader in starting churches in Ephesus, Smyrna, Pergamum, Thyatira, Sardis, Philadelphia, Laodicea, Colossae, and Hierapolis. There were many churches that were birthed out by other leaders following the same gospel that Paul preached. The point to this is that obedience to spiritual instructions from God means following him.

Although obeying God sometimes leads to one becoming a leader in a particular area, that person does not get to that leadership role before first following God's instructions. For example, to become a pastor, one must first be called by God. *Jeremiah 3:15* says,

> And I will give you pastors according to mine heart, which shall feed you with knowledge and understanding.

After the call, the individual starts to follow God's Word of how to live as a pastor.

> If any be blameless, the husband of one wife, having faithful children not accused of riot or unruly. (Titus 1:6)

And of course, there are many more instructions the Bible gives to be an effective pastor. This holds true for any spiritual position that God allows one to hold.

> The husbandman that laboureth must be first partaker of the fruits. (2 Timothy 2:6)

Following the qualifications of becoming a spiritual leader does not end the following process. Once you have stepped into the role, you must be willing and obedient to follow in the areas of what it takes to be successful in that position. For instance, if you are called to be a leader in the church, you must follow God's guidance on how he wants you to carry out that role. Since you will be leading people, you need to know how to follow the concerns of the people. You follow by having a listening ear, having a concerned heart, and being patient and attentive to the people's needs. If Moses didn't possess a listening ear, love in his heart, and patience for God's people, he would not have even gotten out of the outskirts of the Egyptian borders. Although the people complained, Moses followed up on the legitimate concerns by consulting God's directions in prayer. God even instructed Samuel to hear the people's concern on their desire to have a king in *1 Samuel 8:5–7:*

> And said unto him, Behold, thou art old, and thy sons walk not in thy ways: now make us a king to judge us like all the nations. But the thing displeased Samuel, when they said, Give us a king to judge us. And Samuel prayed unto the Lord. And the Lord said unto Samuel, Hearken unto the voice of the people in all that they say unto thee: for they have not rejected thee, but they have rejected me, that I should not reign over them.

Jesus had a great concern as to what the people thought about him. He asked the disciples in *Matthew 16:13–19,*

> And Jesus went out, and his disciples, into the towns of Caesarea Philippi: and by the way he asked his disciples, saying unto them, Whom do men say that I am? And they answered, John the Baptist; but some say, Elijah; and others, One of the prophets. And he saith unto them, But whom say ye that I am? And Peter answereth and saith unto him, Thou art the Christ.
>
> When Jesus came into the coasts of Caesarea Philippi, he asked his disciples, saying, Whom do men say that I the Son of man am? And they said, Some say that thou art John the Baptist: some, Elias; and others, Jeremias, or one of the prophets. He saith unto them, But whom say ye that I am? And Simon Peter answered and said, Thou art the Christ, the Son of the living God. And Jesus answered and said unto him, Blessed art thou, Simon Barjona: for flesh and blood hath not revealed it unto thee, but my Father which is

in heaven. And I say also unto thee, That thou art Peter, and upon this rock I will build my church; and the gates of hell shall not prevail against it. And I will give unto thee the keys of the kingdom of heaven: and whatsoever thou shalt bind on earth shall be bound in heaven: and whatsoever thou shalt loose on earth shall be loosed in heaven.

He knew who he was and why he came, but it was important that the people understood who he was and the important reasoning for his coming. When Peter stated that he was the Christ, this started the whole meaning of the revolution of following Christ, God's son. It also established the Word, which was the foundation for the people that would inherit eternal life.

Following up is a mandatory job of a leader. A leader does not leave situations hanging in the rafters, hoping that things will work themselves out. Instead, a leader searches for what is needed to complete the task at hand. Any problem that is posed to a leader demands that the person do all within the power that God gives them to produce a solution. A leader does not reach the height of their capability first before they begin following the path of God's directions. Instead, a leader follows what is said in *Proverbs 3:6*:

> In all thy ways acknowledge him, and he shall direct thy paths.

This means to follow the direction in which God takes you.

Leading to follow in spiritual situations is a humbling process. Because you are dealing in spiritual things, it takes away from your ability to randomly make and enforce decisions of your intellect.

> For my thoughts are not your thoughts, neither are your ways my ways, says the LORD. (Isaiah 55:8)

The very idea or solution that you plan to present could be the spiritual death of the situation.

> There is a way that seems right to a man, But its
> end is the way of death. (Proverbs 14:12)

Allowing your spirit to follow God's direction will illuminate any kind of spiritual catastrophe that the devil has plotted.

Leading in spiritual situations does not always mean that the answer to a problem or an idea for the people will always be given to you. Sometimes God speaks to others about the situation, and it is relayed to you by the person that God has spoken to. As a good leader, you must be willing to humble yourself and follow the direction that was given by God. In the NET Bible, *Hebrews 3:15* says,

> As it says, "Oh, that today you would listen as
> he speaks! Do not harden your hearts as in the
> rebellion."

God uses who he chooses to get the message across to his people. If you cannot follow while in a leadership position, you will miss the very reason why God allowed you to obtain the position. And let us not forget what happens when we get too big to follow God's leading; remember Nebuchadnezzar in Daniel 4:33? Do not think that you got here on your own? No. It was by the grace of God.

David was one of the greatest warriors for God's people, but he never went up in a battle without first consulting God and following his directions.

> So David asked God, "Should I go out to fight
> the Philistines? (1 Chronicles 14:10)

> Then David asked the LORD, "Should I chase
> after this band of raiders? And when David

inquired of the Lord, he said, "You shall not go up." (1 Samuel 30:8)

Although David knew that God highly favored him, he never took it for granted or struck out on his own leading. He knew that following God would lead to success. He trained himself to follow spiritually by seeking God in all his decisions. He trusted God in tending the sheep, destroying Goliath, and even seeking God's direction on how to bring the ark of the covenant into the city. You will find spiritual success and growth in your leadership role when you submit to following God's direction.

CHAPTER 2

Dealing with People

Moses certainly showed us the ins and outs, ups and downs, and consequences we face when dealing with people whether they are the "Pharaohs" or "God's people." This is a task that requires a great deal of *prayer* and *humility* because without these attributes, you will not hear from God nor follow his instructions. Also, you will not be successful in your endeavors of dealing with the people God has placed in your care or path.

Prayer is the key to dealing with people whether they are God's elect in salvation or sinners in the world. You as a leader must *follow* the promptings and unctions from the Holy Ghost when he is leading you into prayer.

> But ye have an unction from the Holy One, and
> ye know all things. (1 John 2:20)

Prayer opens the mind of a leader to follow God's leadership. Let's look at Jesus. He conquered the keys of death and hell.

> I am he that liveth, and was dead; and, behold, I
> am alive for evermore, Amen; and have the keys
> of hell and of death. (Revelation 1:18)

With that victory, He has given us those same keys to be victorious here on earth.

And I will give unto thee the keys of the kingdom of heaven: and whatsoever thou shalt bind
on earth shall be bound in heaven: and whatsoever thou shalt loose on earth shall be loosed in
heaven. (Matthew 16:19)

But to do this, Jesus was prayerful.

And he withdrew himself into the wilderness and
prayed. (Luke 5:16)

He was subject to the Father in heaven.

And when all things shall be subdued unto him,
then shall the Son also himself be subject unto
him that put all things under him that God may
be all in all. (1 Corinthians 15:28)

He stated that he came to do the Father's will.

For I came down from heaven, not to do mine
own will, but the will of him that sent me. (John
6:38)

When we are dealing with people and their issues, prayer is a
must. There is no way around it.

And he spake a parable unto them to this end,
that men ought always to pray, and not to faint.
(Luke 18:1)

If you faint, you will then cease to "follow the leader," which is
God. If Jesus would not have been subject to the Father, he would
not have been able to complete the task he was chosen to do. Jesus
understood that he was a servant of the Father. He knew that he was

to die for the sins of the people, but he never lost sight of the fact that the Father was the one that would raise him from the dead.

> And God hath both raised up the Lord, and will also raise up us by his own power. (1 Corinthians 6:14)

In the Bible, God says,

> Behold, all souls are mine; as the soul of the father, so also the soul of the son is mine: the soul that sinneth, it shall die. (Ezekiel 18:4)

God even knows the number of hairs that are on our head even after the hairs fall out and grow back.

> But even the very hairs of your head are all numbered. (Luke 12:7)

Since God knows all about us, wouldn't it be better to listen to him and follow what he says to do when dealing with people? A leader must remember that these are God's people and that he is only allowing you, the leader, to be the servant in their lives in the earth realm. Even in the secular world, bosses and supervisors must remember that the people they are entrusted to lead do not work for them but for the company or agency that hired them. In the secular world, there are rules and regulations that leaders must *follow* while in a leadership position over the employees of that business. In dealing with people, if we do not follow instructions on how to lead, pride can set up in the leader. Prayer is the key to the heart, and it unlocks the door of pride.

Pride often tries to attack the hearts of leaders whether it's in the church or the secular world. If pride locks itself onto the heart of a leader, the possibility of successfully dealing with people will be a failure. In the Bible, God did not take prideful leaders so well.

Nebuchadnezzar was one of God's greatest examples of how he deals with prideful leaders.

> The king spake, and said, Is not this great Babylon, that I have built for the house of the kingdom by the might of my power, and for the honour of my majesty? While the word was in the king's mouth, there fell a voice from heaven, saying, O king Nebuchadnezzar, to thee it is spoken; The kingdom is departed from thee. And they shall drive thee from men, and thy dwelling shall be with the beasts of the field: they shall make thee to eat grass as oxen, and seven times shall pass over thee, until thou know that the most High ruleth in the kingdom of men, and giveth it to whomsoever he will. The same hour was the thing fulfilled upon Nebuchadnezzar: and he was driven from men, and did eat grass as oxen, and his body was wet with the dew of heaven, till his hairs were grown like eagles' feathers, and his nails like birds' claws. (Daniel 4:30–33)

No matter how tempting it is to follow your own desires when dealing with people, it is not your realm to do so. Remember, you are a good follower—a good follower of God's leading.

CHAPTER 3

Making Everyday Decisions

To do or not to do!—You face this statement in every decision you make.

You ask these questions:

- God, is this your will?
- Will God be pleased in this decision?
- How do I know I am making the right choice?
- What is the right choice?
- Who will be affected by this decision?

You begin to sound like an old familiar church quote:

Questions, questions, on my mind, will the Lord
be pleased this time?

Well, when you are a leader with good following skills, you don't have to ponder over the above questions. Your answers will come in your willingness to follow what God tells you personally and in His Word. That's right, personally! Sometimes, depending on your situation of the decision being made, God will visit you personally in the spirit. The answer to some decisions does not always present itself clear to you from the Bible. You can read a passage over and over, but the answer to what you are seeking does not always jump out at you. You can read, pray, and meditate, yet find to no avail an answer.

That's when you know that God is going to visit you spiritually with the answer he wants you to follow. Don't fret, the answer is not yet. Wait on the Lord, and he will come through.

The church

One of the biggest mistakes church leaders make is thinking they are *the* voice in the lives of God's people. But church leaders are *a* voice for the people of God. Oh yeah, there is a difference between *the* and *a*. "*A* voice in the lives of God's people" is the directions given to them by the leader, who has received from God what to tell them. "*The* voice for their lives" is God's word for the directions they are to take that will ultimately direct and affect them. Let us go back to Moses. He was the leader for God's people. He was *a* voice for God's people in delivering *the* message to them that was directed by God. In other words, he followed the instructions God gave him for the people by telling the people what God wanted them to do, such as in *Exodus 13:23*:

> And the LORD went before them by day in a pillar of
> a cloud, to lead them the way; and by night in a pillar
> of fire, to give them light; to go by day and night.

This was God's instructions on how he would lead his people through the wilderness. So Moses relayed this message to them. Now, to survive through the wilderness, the people had to obey the instructions given to them by Moses for their survival. Their lives were directed and affected by the instructions that were given by God. You see, Moses didn't provide the route; the pillar of cloud and the pillar of fire directed the route. He was the mouthpiece that gave instructions to the people from God for their travel through the wilderness. Get it! Another situation where God worked in the lives of his people is where Moses spoke to the people to direct them, in Numbers 21:9:

> So, Moses made a bronze serpent, and put it on
> a pole; and so it was, if a serpent had bitten any-

one, when he looked at the bronze serpent, he
lived.

Obedience to the instructions for the people given by Moses caused the effect of healing in their lives. Moses did not do the healing, nor did he come up with the decision for them to look at the bronze serpent. What was manifested in this situation came about because a leader followed the instructions of God. The leader does not have to ponder over what decision to make themselves. God knows everything, but as leaders, you must remember the fact that *God knows everything*.

This does not and in no way diminish your responsibility to make decisions in your role as a leader. You are to *follow* the instructions that God gives you to be a good leader in whatever area you are placed. If you are a pastor, you know the instructions from God in that position. The Bible says,

> And I will give you shepherds according to My
> heart, who will feed you with knowledge and
> understanding. (Jeremiah 3:15)

You follow what God says and feed God's people. For example, if you are a leader in the decision-making of the choir, you know you will have to seek out and follow what is needed to lead the choir. You do not have to have a mountain experience like Moses to make certain decisions in the church, just be the mountain that is willing to follow the instructions that God has placed inside you. God will not put more on you than you can bear (i.e., more than you can accomplish). He chose you for the leadership position because of your willingness to follow. So decision-making was one of the benefits that was placed in you by Him.

Your home

> One who rules his own house well, having his children in submission with all reverence (for if a man does not know how to rule his own house, how will he take care of the church of God?). (1 Timothy 3:4–5)

The same way you follow God's instructions to lead in the church, you must do likewise in your own home. Remember, the people in your home are God's people too, same people, different location! Sometimes leaders will strive to perfect leadership in the church but will never seek God's instructions to be a leader in their home. The above scripture states, "One who rules his own house." All Bible translations for the word *rules* in this verse is translated to mean "manage."

> He must *manage* his own family well and see that his children obey him, and he must do so in a manner worthy of full respect. (NIV; emphasis added)

> He must *manage* his own family well, having children who respect and obey him. (NLT; emphasis added)

> He must *manage* his own household well, with all dignity keeping his children submissive. (ESV; emphasis added)

> He must be one who *manages* his own household well, keeping his children under control with all dignity. (NASB; emphasis added)

> One who *manages* his own household competently, having his children under control with all dignity. (HCSB; emphasis added)

> He must *manage* his own family well and have children who are submissive and respectful in every way. (ISV; emphasis added)

To manage something, you must make decisions. And if you are managing your home life according to the Scripture, you must be following the directions of God in your decision-making. If not, you will be making a mess.

Leading to follow in your home life opens the door to a healthy and godly relationship within the structure of the family. Dominance and control only shuts up pain, hurt, questions, and a lack of trust. When you follow the route of a situation to get to the root of the matter, you allow an avenue that will help you see better into what is going on in a particular situation or area. Sometimes you must *follow* a conversation or statement to see where it leads and decide how to apply a solution. Sometimes you will have to see a thing through and allow it to work itself out—such as when children don't agree about something minor. Someone once told me that they "pick their battles." This tells me that you don't have to seek for a decision in everything because sometimes it is not worth it. I guess that's where this scripture comes in:

> And we know that *all things work together* for good to those who love God, to those who are the called according to His purpose. (Romans 8:28; emphasis added)

The door that leads to a good example of a good follower starts with,

> The hardworking farmer must be first to partake of the crops. (2 Timothy 2:6 NKJV)

This is a good example of showing "If you can take it, you can make it." Your home is one of the most important areas where good followers are birthed into good leaders. *Following* your own teaching and disciplines in your home shows your tenacity to follow outside the home. If you set rules in the home, you must first follow them yourself. Always expecting others to do what you dare not even try to do shows hypocritical guidelines. The old familiar saying "Do as I say and not as I do" does not wash these days. Your family wants to see you follow the same rules and examples that you have set. When Paul said, "Follow me and I follow Christ," he literally really meant that whether it be in your home or church. Being a good follower of your own rules at home shows your willingness to do what is right, not just to show who is the boss. To be honest with you, you are not the boss over your life anyway whether it's in or outside the home.

> Or do you not know that your body is the temple of the Holy Spirit who is in you, whom you have from God, and you are not your own? For you were bought at a price; therefore glorify God in your body and in your spirit, which are God's. (1 Corinthians 6:19–20) ESV

God glories in seeing a true child of his going in the direction or path that has been set before them. But to see his child going in the direction that persuades others to follow because of their faithfulness to follow Him, it gives God a greater glory. Some people think that committing themselves to a life of partaking of your own fruit (which means humbling down under your own rules set in the home) is meant to be a weakness. They may say, "How can you be a leader outside your home when you are humbling down in your own home?" But you are a good leader because you realize that good leadership is not how hard you push others into following the rules and guidelines, but it is predicated upon how well you follow those same rules and guidelines.

One of the best ways to be a good follower at home lies in your desire and drive to let your family know your willingness and determination to follow what is right behind the closed doors of your home. Some people put on a good public display but do not exemplify any temperance with their family when it comes to following what they preach. Sometimes yelling and demanding others in the home only causes a lack of trust within the home. Lack of trust takes harmony from the home. For example, your family should be able to depend upon promises you make. You should always follow up and keep your word. Never put a strong demand on your family to follow you somewhere you don't even follow Christ. Your commitment to follow Christ, even in your home, allows your family to take extra steps to follow you. When your family can see you following with great sacrifices, they will want to join and sacrifice as well. We are all the family of Christ. We are one body, and he is our head; therefore, we follow his leading and guiding.

Love is the key ingredient in the home, and it is following the directions of Christ in his instructions in *John 13:34*:

> A new commandment I give to you, that you
> love one another; as I have loved you, that you
> also love one another.

One must *follow* the guidelines of love in the home to be effective in leading the family. Love allows one to follow the rules of forgiveness. It will also lead you to follow the rest of what is listed as the fruit of the spirit: joy, peace, forbearance, kindness, goodness, faithfulness, gentleness, and self-control. Putting on these attributes helps eliminate seeing and criticizing everyone else's shortcomings and will allow you to follow what the Word of God is saying to you. This will help you be a good follower even in your own personal life.

CHAPTER 4

Your Personal Life

I'm sure you have often heard the cliché, "I am 3 × 7 plus," meaning "I am twenty-one-plus years old." This is often used when someone wants to get the point across that they have become an adult and can make their own decisions. But in this walk of life, you have been bought with a price, and that means *following* where God leads you.

> For ye are bought with a price: therefore, glorify
> God in your body, and in your spirit, which are
> God's. (1 Corinthians 6:20)

Newsflash: You are not your own. So fall in line and start following the leadership of the Lord. Go where he says to go. Stop when he says stop. Listen, listen, and listen for his instructions for your life.

Some leaders will consult God for instructions for the church, their communities, their job, and even their family. But somewhere along the line, they never take out the time to consult God for their own personal lives. Saints, friends, and loved ones who are reading this book, please, please take the time to hear what God is saying to you in his instructions that you are to follow in your personal life. Don't go on your own directions. For the Bible says in *Proverbs 14:12,*

> There is a way which seemeth right unto a man,
> but the end thereof are the ways of death.

Following your own desired way can lead to not just physical death but also spiritual death. Yes, being headstrong can lead to physical death. For example, a person that never listens to God regarding things in their personal life—such as health, their temper, eating habits, and so forth—can lead them to physical death. Remember, warning comes before destruction.

> Pride goeth before destruction, and an haughty
> spirit before a fall. (Proverbs 16:18)

Pride is the main sin that allows a person to keep on in their ways and not follow the instructions of God. The same goes for spiritual death. You must follow what God is saying to you to remain spiritually alive with him. The Holy Spirit was sent to lead and guide us in all truth.

> Howbeit when he, the Spirit of truth, is come,
> he will guide you into all truth: for he shall not
> speak of himself; but whatsoever he shall hear,

that shall he speak: and he will shew you things
to come. (John 16:13)

God instructs us through the Spirit. The Holy Spirit is in us, and it testifies of Christ.

But when the Comforter is come, whom I will
send unto you from the Father, even the Spirit of
truth, which proceedeth from the Father, he shall
testify of me. (John 15:26)

The Spirit itself beareth witness with our spirit,
that we are the children of God. (Romans 8:16)

If the Holy Ghost is prompting you to do something, then you need to follow that leading. It is the voice of God. The Bible says in *John 2:27*,

But the anointing which ye have received of him
abideth in you, and ye need not that any man
teach you: but as the same anointing teacheth
you of all things, and is truth, and is no lie, and
even as it hath taught you, ye shall abide in him.

This means that God's spirit in you is your guide. Follow it!

Let's use the scenario of a car that you purchase. The car manufacturer makes the car. They then sell the car to the dealership. The dealership sells the car to you. The bank finances the car, and you pay the bank. When you pay off the car from the finance company, the car is yours. There is a long process in obtaining the car, but it finally becomes yours. But what is constant in this whole process is, at the time you obtain the car from the dealership, you determine where the car goes. You make the decision to drive or park the car. The car does not get up and go where it wants to go because you are still paying the bank loan. The minute you become the possessor of the car, it must obey and follow your instructions. Why? Because you are owner, the possessor of it. The bank does not tell the car where to go. You are paying the payments to possess and control the car. Well, this is the same way with your life. God made you. Christ died for you. The Holy Spirit possesses you and instructs you because you belong to God. When you were a sinner, you belonged to the devil; therefore, you did what the devil said to do. The devil instructed you and led you into sin, and you obeyed. Now you have changed ownership, which is God, so you now *follow* him. There is never a time that your life is your own to do with it what you see fit.

CHAPTER 5

Conclusion

I did not give the definition of *follow*. Why? God wanted you to first understand the attributes of following. He wanted you to understand the importance of following and how it affects you as a leader and the ability to lead.

Follow means "to go or come after," "move or travel behind," and "come after in time or order." Yes, he saved the best for last. Most leaders do not want to move behind or come after. But seeing the effects that following has on effective leadership, it puts you in the willingness to follow. Sometimes leaders do not start out on a leadership journey expecting to follow behind. There is that assumption to always be up front. But God is saying in this book, "When you fall behind and see things from behind, you will see the effects of your leadership." Waiting first on God will help you not make hasty, destructive decisions. Hearing the conclusion of the matter and getting a full understanding can help you to avoid many errors in your leadership role. This is not to say you will not make mistakes, stumble, and learn many things. But when you follow God and obey his instructions, if you err, you soon correct the problem and move on with the tenacity to keep going. Your strength and hope do not come from you but from God, and there is no failure in God. When a leader ceases to follow, it opens an area in their leadership role that blocks their view of seeing their errors, which need to be corrected.

In the definition of *follow* that states, "To come after in time and order," this allow you to move in the right timing. Our timing is not God's timing; therefore, we should follow his timing. Let him go first, and we follow. The picture on the cover of this book says, "Lead to Follow" Leaders need to follow the Shepherd (Christ our Lord), then others will follow us to an expected end, not destruction. Paul pins it best in 1 Corinthians 11:1.

Be ye followers of me, even as I also am of Christ.

May God keep and bless you!

A Church Birthed Out of Toil and Tribulation

When I started writing this book, I did not know that God was positioning me to be birthed through what I was about to experience. Just before the ending of writing this book, God allowed me to go through a series of trials and tribulations through the process of learning to follow his directions. God gave me instructions in areas of my spiritual life that I had never experienced. He allowed me to meet people and go to places that were unfamiliar to me. The only way I could survive spiritually was to follow his guidance. The toil came with the constant questioning of his will. I did not understand why I was given difficult tasks to complete in my spiritual walk. The tribulation came with experiencing resentment because of the walk that I had to complete according to God's instructions. But through it all, I made it. I stood back, looked over my life, and said, "Thank you, Lord. You brought me through it." When you learn to *follow* God's leadership, you will prevail. You will come out like the Israelites; your shoes will not wear out.

> And I have led you forty years in the wilderness: your clothes are not waxen old upon you, and thy shoe is not waxen old upon thy foot. (Deuteronomy 29:5)

I call it *birthed out* because it made me a new person. I was the church already, but the birthing out created a new church. Listening and obeying God's instructions taught me *not* to pick *my* battles but allow him to fight *the* battles. Remember, *the* battle is not yours. In the process of being made over, you realize that you are not your own; therefore, the toils of this life are not yours. We are ambassadors that have been chosen to be a part of this world, but not of this world, to spread the good news of Christ. When we refuse to listen and follow God's leadership, we become stagnant in a world that is not our home. Ambassadors follow leadership rules from the country that they are a citizen of. Since we are royal priests of the kingdom of God, do not allow this world to dictate your assignment.

SOURCES

The following list is a collection of the sources used for this book:

- *Merriam-Webster Dictionary*
- *NET Translation Bible*
- Strong's Greek Translation
- The Holy Bible (King James Version)
- *Wikipedia Online Encyclopedia*

ABOUT THE AUTHOR

In 1996, Minister Mary Griffin made the decision to accept Christ back into her life and live a life of holiness. She didn't realize at that time that the decision was not wholly hers but that God was calling her and preparing her for what was to come later in her life because without him, she could not have made this journey. Mary started her master's program in 1999 and completed the coursework in December 2002 while raising three grandchildren. She received her master's degree in criminal justice from Florida A&M University. She was called into the ministry in 2009. Her passion is evangelism. She performs door-to-door witness, does Bible reading to residents at nursing homes, and delivers tracks daily to every soul she can reach. Mary remembers and lives by the words of the late Bishop E. L. Sheppard from Quincy, Florida, in which he stated, "Whatever you are given to do, do it well. If you are a ditch digger, dig the ditch to the best of your ability. Try to perfect anything that has been given charge to your hands."

> All things work together for good to them that
> love God, to them who are the called according
> to his purpose. (Romans 8:28)

God blessed me with a saved and holy husband, Brother Darred Griffin. We witness together on the street corners and distribute tracks. We must have the faith and trust the things we cannot see.

www.ingramcontent.com/pod-product-compliance
Lightning Source LLC
Chambersburg PA
CBHW040205160726
48006CB00014B/1903